picnics

picnics

simple recipes for eating outdoors

RYLAND
PETERS
& SMALL

LONDON NEW YORK

First published in Great Britain in 2005
by Ryland Peters & Small
20–21 Jockey's Fields
London WC1R 4BW
www.rylandpeters.com

10 9 8 7 6 5 4 3 2 1

Printed in China

ISBN 1 84172 815 2

A CIP record for this book is available
from the British Library.

Senior Designer Steve Painter
Commissioning Editor
Elsa Petersen-Schepelern
Editor Sharon Cochrane
Production Sheila Smith
Picture Research Tracy Ogino
Art Director Gabriella Le Grazie
Publishing Director Alison Starling

Notes
• All spoon measurements are level
unless otherwise specified.
• All eggs are medium unless otherwise
specified. Uncooked or partly cooked
eggs should not be served to the very
young, the very old, those with
compromised immune systems or
to pregnant women.
• Before baking, weigh or measure all
ingredients exactly and prepare baking
tins or sheets.
• Ovens should be preheated to the
specified temperature.

contents

the perfect picnic

Choose a spot for your picnic that's easy to get to, preferably close to where you can park the car. It's all very well planning a romantic picnic at the top of a mountain, but don't forget that a picnic basket can get very heavy, very quickly!

comfort

• If you are travelling by car, take light, collapsible tables and chairs.

• Take plenty of rugs and cushions.

• Choose a shady place to spread your picnic blanket.

• Pack lanterns, torches and citronella tea-lights if you will still be outside in the evening.

storage

• Safety and convenience are the most important elements when it comes to packing the food.

• Use cool bags or boxes. Pack the base with freezer blocks and put raw ingredients on the bottom and more delicate ones on top. This is also the best method for carrying ice cubes.

• Refrigerate precooked or prepared food until ready to pack.

• Remove marinated meat or fish from the refrigerator 1 hour before cooking to let it return to room temperature. It will cook more quickly, reducing the risk of undercooking and spoiling.

• Chill and store the food in the same container; plastic containers, zip lock bags and Thermos flasks are all good. Plastic or glass bottles are ideal for drinks, dressings or syrups.

• Wrap sandwiches and rolls in baking parchment, then in foil. Store and transport cakes in their tins.

• Hardware and office supply stores sell aluminium storage tins. Cookware shops and Asian stores also sell stackable stainless-steel lunch boxes – ideal for small snack dishes.

• Remember to take along a bag in which to bring home any rubbish after the picnic.

transport

• Picnic baskets are romantic, but often impractical. When full, they're very heavy and difficult for one person to carry. Two-handled baskets are preferable because you can share the load.

• Use paper plates and plastic beakers – or glasses and plates wrapped individually in kitchen paper or cloth to avoid breakage.

• For adventurous picnic destinations, pack non-perishable foods that can be eaten with your fingers to save having to carry a heavy pack. A backpack is the easiest way to transport lunch if you are walking a long distance or going up or down steep hills.

market picnic

Menu suggestions

Parma ham

salami

potato and tarragon cake

mixed washed leaves

pâté en croûte

sliced ham and parsley mousse

pissaladière

bread

goats' cheese

peaches

chocolate opera cake

apple custard tart

hazelnut biscuits

vanilla yoghurts

To drink

apple cider

old-fashioned lemonade

market shopping

If you don't have the time to cook what you need for your picnic, or you just fancy spoiling yourself, visit your local market or farmers' market. Sometimes the producers are on the stalls selling their own goods, so you can chat about what is on offer. It's such a treat, as well as being a very sensual experience, to shop for food in a market. It often looks so raw and real, with the stallholders full of stories and love for their produce. Don't be afraid to ask questions – they invariably have a wealth of information that they are often only too happy to share.

The menu on the left is just to give you an idea of what you can buy from a market to create an instant, no-cook picnic. Delicacies will vary from place to place, but it's always fun to be adventurous and try something that you're not familiar with, be it a cheese, pâté, tart or simply an unusual bread.

the scene

After gathering your purchases together in baskets, boxes and bags, you will need to find a quiet, shady spot for you to set up your picnic. Spread out a blanket or large, pretty cloth and put out all the delicious produce on it for everyone to unwrap. Sit back and enjoy your no-cook *al fresco* feast.

the style

This is really dictated by the surroundings and the goods you buy. Some producers take such pride in their packaging and presentation – beautiful sheets of waxed paper to wrap meats and cheeses, pretty boxes to protect tarts and cakes, crisp, paper bags for bread and pretty baskets for fruit. All you need is a beautiful picnic blanket or cloth on which to set out your feast, as well as cutlery, glasses, napkins and the all-important corkscrew.

Chickpeas are a fantastic ingredient, but unfortunately most people don't really know what to do with them. Buying canned chickpeas, as in this super Mediterranean style salad, makes them so easy to use.

5 plum tomatoes, halved and deseeded

3 large red peppers, halved and deseeded

375 g canned chickpeas, rinsed and drained

a bunch of flat leaf parsley

sea salt and freshly ground black pepper

extra virgin olive oil, to serve

Serves 4

chickpea, tomato and pepper salad

Lightly oil a roasting tin and put the tomatoes and peppers in it. Cook in a preheated oven at 190°C (375°F) Gas 5 for 20 minutes.

Remove from the oven and transfer the tomatoes and peppers to a bowl. Add the drained chickpeas, then stir in the parsley and season with salt and pepper. Let cool.

Transfer the salad to an airtight container. When you are ready to eat, sprinkle with a little olive oil and serve.

salads and vegetarian

broad bean salad with mint and parmesan

Great for picnics, this salad can also be served as part of a tapas spread, as a starter or snack. If it's early in the season and you have young, tender broad beans, it's not necessary to peel them after blanching. If you can't get hold of fresh broad beans, use frozen ones or runner beans cut into 3 cm lengths.

750 g podded, young fresh or frozen broad beans

3 heads of chicory

leaves from 3 sprigs of mint

25 g Parmesan cheese

Hazelnut oil dressing

2 tablespoons extra virgin olive oil

4 tablespoons hazelnut oil*

2 teaspoons white wine vinegar

1 teaspoon Dijon mustard

¼ teaspoon sugar

sea salt and freshly ground black pepper

Serves 6

Plunge the broad beans into a saucepan of lightly salted, boiling water, return to the boil and simmer for 1–2 minutes. Drain and refresh the beans immediately under cold running water. Pat dry with kitchen paper and peel away the grey-green outer skin if necessary. Put the peeled beans in a large airtight container.

Cut the chicory in half lengthways, slice thickly crossways, then add to the beans. Add the mint leaves, tearing any large ones in half. Using a potato peeler, cut thin shavings of Parmesan over the salad.

Put all the dressing ingredients in a screw-top jar and shake well to mix.

Just before serving, shake the dressing well and sprinkle it over the salad. Toss well and serve.

*Note If hazelnut oil is difficult to find, substitute extra virgin olive oil. Buy nut oils in small quantities and store them in the refrigerator: they are delicate and become rancid very quickly.

This satisfying summer salad with a delicious hint of fresh mint is a superb accompaniment to cold meat or fish.

courgette, feta and mint salad

1 tablespoon sesame seeds

6 large courgettes

0 tablespoons extra virgin olive oil

150 g feta cheese, crumbled

a handful of fresh mint leaves

sea salt and freshly ground black pepper

Dressing

4 tablespoons extra virgin olive oil

1 tablespoon freshly squeezed lemon juice

1 small garlic clove, crushed

Serves 4

Put the sesame seeds in a dry frying pan and toast over medium heat until golden and aromatic. Remove from the heat, let cool and store in an airtight container.

Cut the courgettes diagonally into thick slices. Put the slices in a bowl, sprinkle with the olive oil, season with salt and pepper and toss well. Cook on a hot stove-top grill pan for 2–3 minutes on each side until charred and tender. Remove from the pan and let cool.

Put all the dressing ingredients in a screw-top jar. Add salt and pepper to taste and shake well.

Put the courgettes, feta and mint in a large airtight container. When ready to serve, shake the dressing and sprinkle it over the salad. Toss well. Sprinkle with the toasted sesame seeds and serve at once.

Ready-made tapenade can be found in supermarkets and delicatessens and is usually quite good quality. Some delis make their own and these are definitely worth seeking out, but make your own if you have the time.

pasta, squash and feta salad with olive dressing

4 tablespoons pumpkin seeds

750 g butternut squash

1 tablespoon extra virgin olive oil

1 tablespoon chopped fresh thyme leaves

500 g dried penne pasta

350 g feta cheese, diced

350 g cherry tomatoes, halved

4 tablespoons chopped fresh basil leaves

sea salt and freshly ground black pepper

Olive dressing

150 ml extra virgin olive oil

3 tablespoons Tapenade (page 35)

freshly squeezed juice of 1 lemon

1 teaspoon clear honey

Serves 6

Put the pumpkin seeds in a dry frying pan and toast over medium heat until golden and aromatic. Remove from the heat, let cool and store in an airtight container.

Peel and deseed the butternut squash and cut the flesh into bite-sized pieces. Put in a bowl or plastic bag and add the oil, thyme, salt and pepper. Toss well, then arrange in a single layer in a roasting tin. Roast in a preheated oven at 200°C (400°F) Gas 6 for about 25 minutes until golden and tender. Let cool.

To make the dressing, put the olive oil, tapenade, lemon juice and honey in a bowl. Whisk well, then add salt and pepper to taste.

Bring a large saucepan of lightly salted water to the boil, add the penne and cook for 8–9 minutes, or according to the timings on the packet, until *al dente* (just cooked but still slightly crunchy in the middle). Drain well, then immediately stir in 4 tablespoons of the dressing. Let cool. Put the remaining dressing in a screw-top jar.

When cool, put the pasta and squash in an airtight container, mix gently, then add the feta cheese, cherry tomatoes and basil. Just before serving, stir in the toasted pumpkin seeds and the remaining dressing.

With its lovely, earthy flavours, a frittata is an Italian version of the Spanish tortilla or the French omelette. Different ingredients are added depending on the region or season.

mixed mushroom frittata

3 tablespoons extra virgin olive oil

2 shallots, finely chopped

2 garlic cloves, finely chopped

1 tablespoon chopped fresh thyme leaves

300 g mixed wild and cultivated mushrooms, such as girolle, chanterelle, portobello, shiitake and cep

6 eggs

2 tablespoons chopped fresh flat leaf parsley

sea salt and freshly ground black pepper

Serves 6

Put 2 tablespoons of the oil in a non-stick frying pan, heat gently, then add the shallots, garlic and thyme. Fry gently for 5 minutes until softened but not browned.

Meanwhile, brush off any dirt clinging to the mushrooms and wipe the caps. Chop or slice coarsely and add to the pan. Fry for 4–5 minutes until just starting to release their juices. Remove the pan from the heat.

Put the eggs in a bowl with the parsley and a little salt and pepper, whisk briefly, then stir in the mushroom mixture. Wipe the frying pan with kitchen paper.

Heat the remaining 1 tablespoon of oil in the clean pan and pour in the egg and mushroom mixture. Cook over medium heat for 8–10 minutes until set on the bottom. Put the pan under a preheated grill and cook the frittata for 2–3 minutes until the top is set and spotted brown. Let cool, then wrap in parchment paper.

Blue cheese and walnuts are a great combination. The Roquefort imparts a richness of flavour to this light creamy tart with walnut pastry.

roquefort and walnut tart

15 g walnuts

100 g plain flour, plus extra for dusting

1 teaspoon salt

50 g butter, chilled and diced

1–2 tablespoons chilled water

Filling

100 g Roquefort cheese, chopped

200 g ricotta cheese

150 ml double cream

3 eggs, lightly beaten

2 tablespoons walnut oil

sea salt and freshly ground black pepper

a tart tin, 23 cm diameter, buttered
baking parchment
baking beans or uncooked rice

Serves 6

To make the pastry, put the walnuts in a dry frying pan and cook for 1–2 minutes over medium heat until they start to smell toasted. Transfer to a bowl and let cool. When cool, transfer to a food processor or blender and grind to a meal. Sift the flour and salt into a bowl and rub in the butter with the tips of your fingers until the mixture resembles fine breadcrumbs. Stir in the ground walnuts. Add the water 1 tablespoon at a time, mixing lightly with a knife to bring the pastry together to form a soft dough. Transfer the dough to a lightly floured work surface, knead gently, then shape into a flat disc. Wrap in clingfilm and chill in the refrigerator for about 30 minutes.

Transfer the dough to a lightly floured work surface, roll out to a disc about 29 cm in diameter and use to line the tart tin. Prick the base of the pastry case all over with a fork and chill for a further 30 minutes.

Line the pastry case with baking parchment and add some baking beans or rice. Bake in a preheated oven at 200°C (400°F) Gas 6 for 10 minutes. Remove the paper and beans or rice and bake for a further 5–6 minutes until the pastry is crisp and lightly golden. Remove from the oven and let cool for 10 minutes. Leave the oven on.

Meanwhile, to prepare the filling, put the Roquefort in a food processor with the ricotta, cream, eggs, walnut oil, salt and pepper. Blend briefly until mixed but not smooth. Pour into the pastry case and cook in the preheated oven for about 20 minutes until risen and golden. Remove from the oven and let cool in the tin.

What is it about caramelized onions? They smell just divine, especially when cooked in butter. These simple onion tarts, topped with creamy goats' cheese, can be eaten warm, although they are also good served cold for picnics.

onion, thyme and goats' cheese tarts

40 g butter

500 g onions, thinly sliced

2 garlic cloves, crushed

1 tablespoon chopped fresh thyme leaves

350 g ready-made puff pastry, defrosted if frozen

flour, for dusting

200 g log of goats' cheese

sea salt and freshly ground black pepper

a baking sheet

Makes 8

Put the butter in a frying pan and melt over low heat. Add the onion, garlic and thyme and fry gently for 20–25 minutes until softened and golden. Season to taste with salt and pepper. Remove the pan from the heat and let cool.

Put the pastry on a lightly floured work surface and roll out to form a rectangle 20 x 40 cm, trimming the edges. Cut the rectangle in half lengthways and into 4 crossways, making 8 pieces in total, each one about 10 cm square.

Divide the onion mixture between the squares, spreading it over the top, leaving a thin border around the edges. Cut the cheese into 8 slices and arrange 1 slice in the centre of each square.

Transfer the pastries to a large baking sheet and bake in a preheated oven at 220°C (425°F) Gas 7 for 12–15 minutes until the pastry has risen and the cheese is golden. Remove from the oven and let cool.

focaccia topped with cherry tomatoes and pesto

The secret to making focaccia is to let the dough rise three times rather than twice, as you would for regular bread dough. It is well worth the extra 30 minutes needed, as the result is light, airy and totally moreish.

15 g fresh yeast or ½ tablespoon easy-blend dried yeast

a pinch of sugar

350 g plain flour, plus extra for dusting

1 teaspoon salt, plus extra for cooking

2 tablespoons extra virgin olive oil, plus extra for drizzling

175 g cherry tomatoes, halved

40 g pitted black olives, halved

Pesto

25 g basil leaves

1 garlic clove, crushed

2 tablespoons pine nuts

6 tablespoons extra virgin olive oil

2 tablespoons freshly grated Parmesan cheese

sea salt and freshly ground black pepper

a baking tin, 20 x 30 cm

Serves 8

If you are using fresh yeast, put it in a small bowl, add the sugar and 225 ml warm water and stir until the yeast has dissolved. Add 2 tablespoons of the flour and leave in a warm place for 10 minutes until frothy. Sift the remaining flour and the salt into a bowl. Add the frothed yeast mixture and oil and mix until a dough forms.

If using easy-blend dried yeast, put the yeast, sugar, flour, salt and oil in a large bowl. Add 225 ml warm water and mix until a dough forms.

Turn out the dough onto a lightly floured work surface and knead for 10 minutes until smooth and elastic. Shape the dough into a ball, transfer to an oiled bowl, cover with clingfilm and let rise in a warm place for 1 hour or until doubled in size.

Transfer the dough to a lightly floured work surface, knead gently, then shape or roll into a rectangle to fit snugly into the baking tin. Cover and let rise for 30 minutes. Use your fingers to make indentations all over the surface of the dough. Cover again and let rise for a further 1 hour until well risen.

Meanwhile, to make the pesto, put the basil, garlic, pine nuts and oil in a food processor and blend to form a vivid green paste. Transfer to a bowl and stir in the Parmesan and salt and pepper to taste.

Spread 2–3 tablespoons of the pesto carefully over the risen dough without letting it collapse. Put the tomatoes and olives on top and sprinkle with a little more oil and about ½ tablespoon salt. Bake in a preheated oven at 200°C (400°F) Gas 6 for about 25 minutes until risen and golden. Remove from the tin and let cool on a wire rack.

breads and dips

Fougasse belongs to the same ancient family of breads as *focaccie*, the original hearth breads. In Provence, these flat, slashed 'ladder breads' (so called because of their shape) are highly decorative and often flavoured with olives or herbs. Their unusual shape makes them easy to pull apart – ideal for picnics.

fougasse

4 tablespoons extra virgin olive oil, plus extra for baking

2 teaspoons honey (optional)

250 g malted wheatgrain flour (or 200 g malted wheatgrain flour plus 50 g buckwheat, triticale or spelt flour)

500 g strong white flour, plus extra for dusting

1 sachet micronized fast-acting yeast, 7 g

2 teaspoons salt

Toppings, your choice of:

sliced garlic

onion rings

black olives, cut into strips

unwaxed orange zest, thinly sliced

orange flower water

2 large baking sheets, oiled

Makes 4 loaves

Put the oil, honey, if using, and 450 ml warm water in a measuring jug and stir to dissolve. Put the flour or flours, yeast and salt in a food processor. With the motor running, pour the liquid through the feed tube to form a dense dough. Stop, then repeat for 30 seconds more, to develop the gluten.

Transfer the dough to a large, oiled bowl, and cover with an oiled plastic bag. Leave in a warm place for at least 30 minutes or up to 2 hours until the dough has doubled in size.

Punch down the risen dough, transfer to a well-floured work surface and knead for 5–8 minutes or until silky and smooth. Return to the bowl, cover as before and let rise again for 20 minutes or until doubled in size, then divide into 4 pieces. Squeeze, pat and knead one ball into an oval. Transfer the oval to an oiled baking sheet and pat or roll it out until it is 3 times its original size and about 1 cm thick. Repeat the process with the second fougasse.

Make 2 rows of diagonal slashes in the dough, then open up the slashes to make larger holes. Tug out at the ends and sides if you would like to open up the dough even more.

Brush the two breads all over with olive oil, then sprinkle with warm water. Add your choice of garlic, onion, olives, orange zest or orange flower water.

Bake each fougasse towards the top of a preheated oven at 220°C (425°F) Gas 7 for 15–20 minutes or until risen, crusty, but still chewy. Repeat with the other 2 portions of dough.

Eat with your fingers, pulling the bread into short lengths.

4 ciabatta rolls

2 garlic cloves, crushed

4 tablespoons extra virgin olive oil

1 tablespoon red wine vinegar

4 ripe tomatoes, thickly sliced

200 g canned tuna in olive oil,
drained and flaked

24 pitted black olives,
preferably niçoise

12 anchovy fillets in oil, drained

2 tablespoons capers

a few rocket leaves

a handful of basil leaves

sea salt and freshly ground
black pepper

Serves 4

Traditionally, pan bagnat, from Nice in the South of France, is made in a large baguette. This recipe uses Italian ciabatta rolls instead, which are slightly easier to transport. They are great for a picnic because they are wrapped in advance and all ready to go.

pan bagnat

Cut the ciabatta rolls in half. Put the garlic, oil and vinegar in a small bowl, mix well, then brush all over the cut surfaces of the rolls.

Divide the remaining ingredients between the 4 rolls, add the lids and wrap in clingfilm. Let the rolls soak and infuse for at least 1 hour before serving.

This loaf packed with grilled vegetables, pesto and goats' cheese is a really tasty alternative to regular sandwiches. Make it a day ahead so it can be pressed overnight in the refrigerator for the flavours to develop and mingle.

stuffed picnic loaf

1 round loaf of bread, about 23 cm diameter, 10 cm high

2 tablespoons extra virgin olive oil

¼ quantity Pesto (page 24)

2 large red onions

2 large red peppers

2 large courgettes

250 g soft goats' cheese, diced

12 large basil leaves

sea salt and freshly ground black pepper

Serves 6

Cut the top off the loaf and carefully scoop out most of the bread, leaving just the outer shell (reserve the bread and use for another dish such as Taramasalata, page 34). Put 1 tablespoon of the oil in a bowl, stir in the pesto and spread half the mixture around the inside of the shell and on the cut side of the lid. Set aside.

Cut the onions into wedges, brush with a little of the remaining oil and cook on a preheated barbecue or on a stove-top grill pan for 10 minutes on each side until very tender. Let cool.

Char-grill the peppers on a preheated barbecue or stove-top grill pan or under a grill for about 15 minutes, turning occasionally, until blackened all over. Transfer to a plastic bag and let cool. Peel away the skin, discard the seeds and cut the flesh into quarters, reserving any juices.

Cut the courgettes lengthways into 2 mm thick slices, brush with oil and barbecue or grill as above for 2–3 minutes on each side until lightly charred and softened. Let cool.

Arrange the cooked vegetables in layers inside the loaf, with the goats' cheese and remaining pesto in the middle and the basil on top. Sprinkle the filling with any remaining oil and the pepper juices and replace the lid.

Wrap the whole loaf in clingfilm and put it on a plate. Put a board on top, then a heavy food can on top of that to weigh it down. Chill in the refrigerator overnight.

The following day, cut into wedges and serve.

4 plain bagels

200 g crème fraîche

2–3 teaspoons wasabi paste

250 g smoked salmon

freshly ground black pepper

To serve (optional)

chopped chives

lemon wedges

Serves 4

A classic American brunch dish given a modern twist with Japanese wasabi paste (horseradish) added to the crème fraîche.

bagels with smoked salmon and wasabi crème fraîche

Cut the bagels in half and toast lightly on both sides. Put the crème fraîche and wasabi paste in a bowl and beat until evenly mixed. Add black pepper to taste.

Spread 4 bagel halves with the wasabi mixture. Top with the smoked salmon and chives, if using, then add the remaining bagel halves. Serve with lemon wedges for squeezing, if using.

taramasalata

Real, home-made taramasalata is a revelation.
It is aeons away from the lurid, tasteless,
manufactured variety sold, alas, worldwide.
The real thing requires salted cod's roe – use
either the uncoloured pressed paste, sold by
authentic Greek delis or grocers, or smoked
and salted roe, sold in the piece, skinned and
chopped (not at all authentic but excellent).
Choose a fruity Greek olive oil for a profoundly
delicious result.

2 tablespoons uncoloured pressed salted cod's roe
or 110 g smoked cod's roe

50 g stale bread, wetted, squeezed dry, then crumbled

freshly squeezed juice of ½ lemon

1 large garlic clove, crushed (optional)

250 ml extra virgin olive oil, preferably Greek

4 tablespoons chopped red onion, blanched

Serves 6–8: makes 400 ml

Put the cod's roe, bread, lemon juice and garlic, if
using, in a food processor. Purée in brief bursts. With
the machine running, drizzle in the oil very slowly
through the feed tube, to form a pale, dense emulsion.
With the machine still running, very gradually drizzle in
3–4 tablespoons of boiling water to lighten the mix.
Stir in the onions. Serve with black olives, raw fennel
or crisp celery pieces, radishes or lettuce hearts and
some torn pita breads.

tapenade

This delicious, intense black paste began life in the South of France as a dip or spread for bread. Capers, anchovy and tuna are essentials and Cognac adds particular pungency.

350 g salt-cured black olives, pitted (250 g after pitting)

50 g anchovy fillets in oil, drained

100 g canned tuna in olive oil, drained

3 garlic cloves, crushed

½ teaspoon dried oregano or marjoram

50 g pickled or salted capers, drained

60 ml extra virgin olive oil

2 tablespoons Cognac

sea salt and freshly ground black pepper

Serves 4–6: makes 500 ml

Put the pitted olives, anchovies, tuna, garlic, oregano or marjoram, capers, salt and pepper in a food processor or mortar and pestle. Work to a messy paste, then drizzle the oil through the feed tube, in pulsing bursts. Taste and adjust the seasoning. Drizzle in half of the Cognac and purée again.

Spoon into an airtight container and drizzle the remaining Cognac over the top.

Serve with crusty bread, croûtes, garlicky bread, crostini, breadsticks or crisp raw vegetables.

hoummus

Lemony, fresh hoummus is a delicious Middle Eastern snack food. For 10-minute hoummus, use canned chickpeas. Excellent olive oil utterly defines the flavour so choose a good one.

200 g dried chickpeas or 400 g canned

freshly squeezed juice of 1 lemon

2 garlic cloves, crushed

¼ teaspoon salt

2 tablespoons tahini paste (optional)

125 ml extra virgin olive oil, plus extra for serving

freshly ground black pepper

hot paprika, to serve

Serves 6–8: makes 400 ml

If using dried chickpeas, put them in a bowl, cover with boiling water and leave for 3 hours (or cover with cold water and leave for 8 hours). Drain. Put in a large saucepan, cover with boiling water, bring back to the boil, part-cover and simmer for 1½–2½ hours or until the chickpeas are easily crushable and tender. Drain.

Put the chickpeas in a food processor with the lemon juice, garlic, salt, pepper and tahini paste, if using. Blend briefly to a mousse. With the machine running, drizzle the oil through the feed tube to form a creamy purée. Taste and add more salt and pepper, if needed.

Serve cool, sprinkled with a little hot red paprika and a trickle of extra virgin olive oil. Serve with crisp lettuce leaves, torn flatbreads and other crisp raw vegetables.

three salsas

Salsas give an extra dimension to chicken, meat and fish and are incredibly versatile.
The hot pineapple and papaya salsa is good with prawns or pork, the creamy corn salsa
marries well with chicken, while the tomato and ginger salsa is very good with white fish
or served as a dip with tortilla chips.

creamy corn salsa

1 ear of fresh corn, husk removed

2 red chillies

1 tomato, diced

1 garlic clove, crushed

freshly squeezed juice of ½ lime

1 tablespoon maple syrup

2 tablespoons sour cream

sea salt and freshly ground black pepper

Serves 6

Preheat a barbecue or grill until hot. Add the corn and cook for about 15 minutes, turning frequently, until charred on all sides. Let cool.

Add the chillies to the barbecue or grill and cook until the skins are charred all over. Transfer to a bowl, cover with a cloth and let cool.

Using a sharp knife, cut down all sides of the corn cob to remove the kernels. Put them in a bowl. Peel and deseed the chillies, chop the flesh and add it to the corn.

Stir in all the remaining ingredients, and add salt and pepper to taste. Transfer to an airtight container.

hot pineapple and papaya salsa

½ ripe pineapple

½ large papaya

freshly squeezed juice of 1 lime

1–2 green chillies, deseeded and chopped

2 spring onions, finely chopped

1 tablespoon chopped fresh mint leaves

1 tablespoon Thai fish sauce

Serves 6

Peel the pineapple, remove and discard the core, then dice the flesh and put in a bowl, together with any juice.

Peel the papaya, scoop out the seeds and dice the flesh. Add to the pineapple.

Stir in the lime juice, chillies, spring onions, mint and fish sauce and set aside to infuse for 30 minutes. Transfer to an airtight container.

tomato, sesame and ginger salsa

2 ripe tomatoes, peeled, deseeded and diced

½ red onion, finely chopped

5 cm fresh ginger, peeled and grated

1 garlic clove, chopped

1 tablespoon chopped fresh coriander

2 tablespoons peanut oil

1 tablespoon soy sauce

1 teaspoon sesame oil

Serves 6

Put all the ingredients in a bowl and stir to mix. Set aside to infuse for about 30 minutes.

Transfer to an airtight container.

chicken caesar wrap

3 large slices of smoked bacon

250 g cooked chicken breast

6 small flour tortillas

300 g cos lettuce, inner leaves only

12 anchovy fillets in oil, drained and chopped

Caesar dressing

1 egg yolk

1 tablespoon freshly squeezed lemon juice

1 teaspoon Worcestershire sauce

150 ml olive oil

25 g freshly grated Parmesan cheese

sea salt and freshly ground black pepper

Serves 6

This salad has travelled all over the world and many additions to the basic lettuce and croûtons with cheese and anchovy dressing can be found. Transforming the salad into a delicious wrap makes a great idea for a picnic dish.

Grill or fry the bacon for 2–3 minutes until crisp. Let cool, then cut into thin strips. Roughly shred the chicken into large strips.

To make the dressing, put the egg yolk in a small bowl, add the lemon juice, Worcestershire sauce and a little salt and pepper and whisk until frothy. Gradually whisk in the oil, a little at a time, until thickened and glossy. Add 2 tablespoons water to thin the sauce, then stir in the grated Parmesan.

Lay a tortilla flat on a work surface and arrange a few lettuce leaves down the middle. Top with chicken, bacon, anchovies, a spoonful of the dressing and, finally, more lettuce. Wrap the tortilla into a roll, then wrap the roll in a napkin. Repeat to make 6 wraps. Chill the wraps in the refrigerator, then transfer to a cool box until ready to serve.

meat and poultry

This really is a great dish – tarragon and chicken go together so well. Kids will love it, yet it tastes good enough for adults to tuck into as well. Pesto can be made out of most herbs, so don't hesitate to try your favourites in this recipe and blend to create your own version. If you don't want meat, replace the chicken with steamed vegetables such as courgettes or runner beans.

300 g dried penne pasta

4 tablespoons olive oil

3 cooked chicken breasts, sliced

100 g rocket

sea salt and freshly ground black pepper

Tarragon pesto

75 g pine nuts

75 g freshly grated Parmesan cheese

a large bunch of tarragon, leaves stripped from the stems and chopped

grated zest and juice of 1 unwaxed lemon

1 garlic clove, finely chopped

5 tablespoons olive oil

Serves 4

chicken and tarragon pesto pasta

Bring a large saucepan of lightly salted water to the boil, add the penne and cook for 8–9 minutes, or according to the timings on the packet, until *al dente* (just cooked but still slightly crunchy in the middle). Drain and refresh the pasta in cold water, then drain thoroughly and toss in the oil.

To make the pesto, put the pine nuts in a dry frying pan and toast over medium heat until golden and aromatic. Remove from the heat and let cool slightly. Put the toasted pine nuts, Parmesan, tarragon, lemon zest and juice, garlic and oil in a jug and, using a hand-held blender, purée until smooth.

Put the pasta, pesto and chicken in a large airtight container. Season with salt and pepper and toss well, coating the pasta and chicken evenly with the pesto. Just before serving, add the rocket to the pasta and toss well (don't add the rocket any earlier because the oil will make it wilt).

This recipe is based on the classic Asian dish salt 'n' pepper squid. It is deliciously fragrant and is sure to appeal to the whole family. Serve with a squeeze of lime and chilli sauce.

pepper 'n' spice chicken

1 small chicken

2 tablespoons toasted sesame oil

1–2 limes, cut into wedges

Sweet Chilli Sauce (page 45), to serve

Fragrant Asian rub

4 whole star anise

2 teaspoons Szechuan peppercorns

1 teaspoon fennel seeds

2 small pieces of cassia bark or 1 cinnamon stick, broken

6 cloves

2 garlic cloves, finely chopped

grated zest of 2 unwaxed limes

1 teaspoon sea salt

Serves 4

To make the rub, put the whole spices in a dry frying pan and toast over medium heat for 1–2 minutes or until golden and aromatic. Remove from the heat and let cool. Transfer to a spice grinder (or clean coffee mill) and crush to a coarse powder. Alternatively, use a mortar and pestle. Transfer the spices to a bowl, add the garlic, lime zest and salt and mix well. Set aside to infuse for about 30 minutes.

Cut the chicken into 12 portions and put in a large dish. Add the rub and sesame oil and work well into the chicken pieces. Cover and let marinate in the refrigerator for 2 hours, but return to room temperature for 1 hour before cooking.

Preheat a barbecue and cook the chicken over medium hot coals, or cook under a preheated medium hot grill, for about 20 minutes, turning after 10 minutes, until the chicken is cooked through. Check by piercing the thickest part of the meat with a skewer – the juices should run clear. Squeeze some lime juice over the chicken and let cool. Serve with the sweet chilli sauce.

chicken sticks with sweet chilli sauce

6 boneless, skinless chicken breasts, cut into 10 cubes each

olive oil, for brushing

Sweet chilli sauce

6 large red chillies, deseeded and chopped

4 garlic cloves, chopped

1 teaspoon grated fresh ginger

1 teaspoon sea salt

100 ml rice wine vinegar

100 g sugar

12 bamboo skewers, soaked in water for about 30 minutes

Serves 12

Chicken sticks are always very popular, so it's worth making extra. You can use boneless chicken thighs, but always remove any excess fat and cook them for a little longer.

To make the sweet chilli sauce, put the chillies, garlic, ginger and salt in a food processor and blend to a coarse paste. Transfer to a saucepan, add the vinegar and sugar, bring to the boil and simmer gently, part-covered, for 5 minutes until the mixture becomes a thin syrup. Remove from the heat and let cool.

Put the chicken cubes and sweet chilli sauce in a bowl and mix well. Cover and chill overnight.

When ready to cook, thread the chicken cubes onto the soaked skewers. Heat the grill to medium-high and brush the rack of the grill pan with oil. Add the chicken sticks to the rack and cook, in batches if necessary, turning frequently, for 15 minutes, or until the chicken is cooked through. Repeat until all the chicken sticks are cooked. Let cool.

mini pork and apple pies

Put the pork fillet, pork belly, bacon and chicken livers in a food processor and blend briefly to mince the meat. Transfer to a bowl and mix in the onion, sage, garlic, nutmeg and a little salt and pepper. Set aside.

To make the pastry, sift the flour and salt into a bowl. Put the fat and 150 ml water in a saucepan and heat gently until the fat melts and the water comes to the boil. Pour the liquid into the flour and, using a wooden spoon, gently draw the flour into the liquid to form a soft dough. Let cool for a few minutes and, as soon as the dough is cool enough to handle, knead lightly in the bowl until smooth.

Divide the dough into 8 equal pieces and roll out 6 of them on a lightly floured work surface to form discs 12 cm across. Carefully invert them, one at a time, over an upturned jam jar. Wrap a 30 x 7 cm piece of waxed paper around the outside, then tie around the middle with kitchen string.

Turn the whole thing over so the pastry is sitting flat. Carefully work the jar up and out of the pastry shell (you may need to slip a small palette knife down between the pastry and the jar, to loosen it).

Divide the pork filling into 6 portions and put 1 portion in each pie. Peel, core and dice the apple and put it on top of the filling. Roll out the remaining 2 pieces of dough and cut 3 rounds from each piece with a pastry cutter, the same size as the top of the pies.

Put a pastry round on top of each pie, press the edges together to seal, then turn the edges inwards and over to form a rim.

To make the glaze, put the egg yolk and milk in a bowl, beat well, then brush over the tops of the pies. Pierce each pie with a fork to let the steam escape, then transfer them to a large baking sheet. Cook in a preheated oven at 190°C (375°F) Gas 5 for 45–50 minutes until golden. Remove from the oven, transfer to a wire rack, let cool and serve cold with a green salad.

250 g pork fillet, diced

125 g pork belly, diced

75 g smoked bacon, diced

25 g chicken livers

1 small onion, minced

1 tablespoon chopped fresh sage

1 small garlic clove, crushed

a pinch of ground nutmeg

1 red apple

1 egg yolk

1 tablespoon milk

sea salt and freshly ground black pepper

Pastry

300 g plain flour

1½ teaspoons salt

60 g white vegetable fat

a jam jar
baking parchment and kitchen string
a baking sheet

Serves 6

Souvlaki is the classic Greek kebab, a delicious combination of cubed lamb marinated in red wine with herbs and lemon juice. The meat is tenderized by the wine, resulting in a juicy and succulent dish.

souvlaki with cracked wheat salad

1 kg neck end of lamb

1 tablespoon chopped fresh rosemary

1 tablespoon dried oregano

1 onion, chopped

4 garlic cloves, chopped

300 ml red wine

freshly squeezed juice of 1 lemon

75 ml olive oil

sea salt and freshly ground pepper

Cracked wheat salad

350 g cracked wheat (bulghur wheat)

25 g fresh flat leaf parsley, chopped

15 g fresh mint leaves

2 garlic cloves, crushed

150 ml extra virgin olive oil

freshly squeezed juice of 2 lemons

a pinch of caster sugar

6 large rosemary stalks or metal skewers

Serves 6

Trim any large pieces of fat from the lamb, then cut the meat into 2.5 cm cubes. Put in a shallow, non-metal dish and add the rosemary, oregano, onion, garlic, wine, lemon juice, olive oil, salt and pepper. Toss well, cover and let marinate in the refrigerator for 4 hours. Return to room temperature for 1 hour before cooking.

To make the salad, soak the cracked wheat in warm water for about 30 minutes until the water has been absorbed and the grains have softened. Strain well to extract any excess water, then transfer to a large airtight container. Add all the remaining ingredients, season to taste with salt and pepper and set aside to develop the flavours.

Thread the lamb onto large rosemary stalks or metal skewers. Cook on a preheated barbecue or under a grill for 10 minutes, turning and basting from time to time. Let rest for 5 minutes, then wrap in foil for transporting. Serve with the salad.

Muffins are quick and easy to prepare and these blueberry ones make a lovely sweet treat for a sunny day. If you don't think a muffin tastes the same without a cup of coffee, put a flask of your favourite brew in the picnic basket.

blueberry and almond muffins

200 g plain flour

1½ teaspoons baking powder

1 teaspoon ground mixed spice

50 g ground almonds

175 g sugar

1 egg

300 ml buttermilk

50 g butter, melted

250 g blueberries

15 g almonds, chopped

12-hole muffin tin with 10 paper muffin cases

Makes 10

Sift the flour, baking powder and mixed spice into a bowl and stir in the ground almonds and sugar. Put the egg, buttermilk and melted butter in a second bowl and beat well. Stir into the dry ingredients to make a smooth batter.

Fold in the blueberries, then spoon the mixture into the muffin cases in the muffin tray until they are three-quarters full. Scatter with the chopped almonds and bake in a preheated oven at 200°C (400°F) Gas 6 for 18–20 minutes until risen and golden. Remove from the oven and let cool on a wire rack. Store in an airtight container and eat within 3 days.

sweet things and drinks

These home-made brownies, deliciously chocolaty and packed with nuts, are real heaven for the taste buds. If you are a true chocoholic, you can top them with a few shavings of white chocolate before serving if you like.

fudge brownies

100 g plain chocolate, finely chopped

125 g unsalted butter, at room temperature

275 g caster sugar

1 teaspoon vanilla essence

2 large eggs, beaten

85 g plain flour

2 tablespoons cocoa powder

a pinch of salt

100 g pecan halves or walnut pieces

a cake tin, 20 cm square, greased and base-lined with baking parchment*

Makes 16

Put the chocolate in a heatproof bowl set over a saucepan of steaming but not boiling water and melt gently (do not let the base of the bowl touch the water). Remove the bowl from the heat and let cool while making the mixture.

Put the butter in a large mixing bowl and, using a wooden spoon or electric mixer, beat until soft and creamy. Add the sugar and vanilla essence and continue beating until the mixture is soft and fluffy. Gradually beat in the eggs.

Sift the flour, cocoa and salt onto the mixture, then spoon the melted chocolate on top and gently stir together until thoroughly mixed. Stir in the nuts. Spoon the mixture into the prepared tin and level the surface.

Bake the brownies in a preheated oven at 180°C (350°F) Gas 4 for 30–35 minutes until a skewer inserted halfway between the sides of the tin and the centre comes out clean – it is important that the centre is just set but still slightly soft and not cake-like. Let cool in the tin, then remove from the tin and cut into 16 squares.

When cold, store the brownies in an airtight container. They are best eaten within 5 days, or can be frozen for up to 1 month.

*Note To make removal easier, cut the parchment paper wider than the tin, so it overlaps the edges. After cooling, remove the uncut slab of brownies using the overlapping paper as handles. Work gently, to avoid cracking the top.

pear gingerbread

500 g self-raising flour

1 tablespoon ground ginger

½ teaspoon bicarbonate of soda

½ teaspoon salt

175 g light soft brown sugar

175 g unsalted butter

175 g black treacle

175 g golden syrup

300 ml milk

1 egg, lightly beaten

2 large pears, peeled, cored and diced

*a baking tin, 30 x 20 cm, greased
and base-lined with baking parchment*

Serves 12

Sift the flour, ginger, bicarbonate of soda and salt into a large bowl. Put the sugar, butter, treacle, golden syrup and milk in a saucepan and heat gently until the butter has melted and the sugar has dissolved. Pour into the flour mixture, then add the egg and beat with a wooden spoon until smooth. Fold in the diced pears, then spoon into the prepared baking tin.

Bake in a preheated oven at 170°C (325°F) Gas 3 for 1½ hours, or until a skewer inserted into the centre comes out clean. Remove from the oven and let cool in the tin for about 10 minutes, then transfer to a wire rack to cool completely.

The cooled cake may be wrapped in foil and stored in an airtight container for up to 5 days.

refrigerator chocolate cake

400 g plain chocolate

125 g unsalted butter

200 g digestive biscuits, coarsely crushed

50 g pine nuts

50 g shelled pistachio nuts, coarsely chopped

100 g crystallized ginger, coarsely chopped

50 g cocoa powder

1 teaspoon ground cinnamon

icing sugar, for dusting (optional)

*a springform cake tin, 23 cm diameter,
greased and base-lined with baking parchment*

Serves 12

Put the chocolate and butter in a heatproof bowl set over a saucepan of steaming but not boiling water and melt gently (do not let the base of the bowl touch the water). Stir in all the remaining ingredients except the icing sugar, then spoon into the prepared cake tin. Press the mixture well into the base and sides of the tin and smooth the surface with a palette knife. Cover with foil and chill overnight in the refrigerator.

When ready to serve, carefully work around the edges of the cake with a palette knife and unmould onto a board, removing the paper from the base. Dust with icing sugar, if using, and cut into thin fingers.

The cake may be stored in the refrigerator for up to 3 days.

Vanilla syrup transforms this cake into a lovely pudding, but you can also serve it simply with a spoonful of yoghurt.

lemon cake with vanilla syrup and strawberries

125 g unsalted butter, softened

125 g caster sugar

grated zest and juice of 2 unwaxed lemons

2 eggs, lightly beaten

200 g self-raising flour

50 g fine semolina

150 ml full-fat plain yoghurt, plus extra to serve (optional)

fresh strawberries, to serve

Vanilla syrup (optional)

150 g caster sugar

1 vanilla pod

a springform cake tin, 23 cm diameter, greased and base-lined with baking parchment

Serves 6

Put the butter, sugar and lemon zest in a bowl and whisk until pale and soft. Gradually beat in the eggs, a little at a time, until evenly mixed. Fold in the flour and semolina, then stir in the yoghurt and lemon juice.

Spoon the mixture into the prepared cake tin and bake in a preheated oven at 180°C (350°F) Gas 4 for about 40 minutes until risen and spongy. The cake is cooked when a skewer inserted into the centre of it comes out clean. Let cool in the tin for 5 minutes, then turn out onto a wire rack to cool completely.

Meanwhile, to make the syrup, if using, split the vanilla pod lengthways. Put the sugar and vanilla pod in a small saucepan and add 300 ml water. Heat gently until the sugar has dissolved. Bring to the boil and simmer for about 5 minutes until it becomes syrupy. Remove from the heat and transfer to a Thermos flask for transporting.

To serve, cut the cake into slices, pour over the syrup and serve with strawberries. Alternatively, serve with yoghurt instead of the syrup.

This cake makes a great treat for picnics and lunchboxes. Feel free to add your favourite nuts or dried fruit instead of the pecans.

toffee loaf cake

250 g plain flour

1 teaspoon bicarbonate of soda

200 g light muscovado sugar

125 ml plain yoghurt

125 ml milk

1 large egg

20 g unsalted butter, melted, plus extra for greasing

50 g chopped pecans, or mixed nuts or sultanas

a loaf tin, 450 g, greased and lined with non-stick baking parchment or greaseproof paper

Makes 1 medium cake

Put the flour, bicarbonate of soda and sugar in a bowl.

Put the yoghurt and milk in a separate bowl. Add the egg and mix with a fork. Add the melted butter. Pour this mixture into the dry ingredients, mix well with a wooden spoon, then stir in the nuts or sultanas.

Spoon the mixture into the prepared tin and bake in a preheated oven at 180°C (350°F) Gas 4 for 45–50 minutes until golden brown. The cake is cooked when a skewer inserted into the centre of it comes out clean.

Remove the tin from the oven and let the cake cool in the tin for 10 minutes. Turn out the cake and transfer to a wire rack to cool completely. Store in an airtight container and eat within 4 days or freeze for up to 1 month. Serve the cake cut into thick slices.

Your dentist won't be happy with this recipe, but you and the kids will be.

nutty toffee apples and toffee cherries

400 g sugar

20 cherries, with stalks

4 apples

100 g chopped nuts

Serves 4

Put the sugar in a small saucepan with 200 ml water and bring to the boil. Reduce the heat and simmer until golden. Do not use a spoon to stir the mixture, just swirl the pan: this keeps the heat even and stops the sugar from crystallizing.

When the caramel is golden, remove the pan from the heat. Holding the stems, quickly dip the cherries into the hot caramel, then put them on a sheet of baking parchment to set.

Spear the apples onto forks. Add the nuts to the caramel and heat through briefly if it is too stiff. Dip the apples in the mixture, swirling them around until coated all over with the nutty caramel. Put on the baking parchment to set for about 5 minutes. Do not let the apples or cherries touch each other or they will stick together.

Wrap the apples and cherries separately in sheets of baking parchment to take to the picnic.

lemonade with mint and bitters

A delightfully simple drink, ideal for hot summer days.

1 litre lemonade

6 sprigs of mint

Angostura bitters

lemon slices

ice cubes

Serves 6

Pour the lemonade into 6 tall glasses, adding a sprig of mint to each one. Add a few drops of bitters, a few slices of lemon and ice cubes to each glass, then serve at once.

iced ginger tea

When making iced tea, it's best to add the tea bags to cold rather than boiling water to avoid the unpleasant scum that can appear on the surface. So boil the water, then let it cool before adding the tea.

50 g fresh ginger, peeled and thinly sliced

4 tea bags

2 limes, sliced

ice cubes

500 ml lemonade

Serves 6

Put the sliced ginger in a large jug, pour over 1 litre boiling water and leave until cold. Add the tea bags and chill in the refrigerator for 1 hour.

Strain the tea into a clean plastic jug with a lid or a thermos flask. Just before serving, add the slices of lime to the tea. Put some ice cubes in 6 glasses, divide the tea between them, and top up with lemonade.

iced lemon coffee

Iced lemon coffee can be just as refreshing as iced lemon tea on a hot day. It may sound a little strange, but it's very thirst-quenching.

500 ml freshly brewed espresso coffee

caster sugar, to taste

ice cubes

1 tablespoon freshly squeezed lemon juice

lemon zest, to serve

Serves 6

Pour the coffee into a large jug, add sugar to taste and stir until dissolved. Let cool, then chill until very cold. Transfer to a Thermos flask to transport.

When ready to serve, half-fill 6 glasses with ice cubes. Add the lemon juice to the coffee, then pour into the glasses and serve with a twist of lemon zest.

index

credits

RECIPES
Louise Pickford
Bagels with smoked salmon and
wasabi crème fraîche
Blueberry and almond muffins
Broad bean salad with mint and
Parmesan
Chicken caesar wraps
Courgette, feta and mint salad
Focaccia topped with cherry
tomatoes and pesto
Iced ginger tea
Iced lemon coffee
Lemonade with mint bitters
Lemon cake with vanilla syrup and
strawberries
Mini pork and apple pies
Mixed mushroom frittata
Onion, thyme and goats' cheese
tarts
Pan bagnat
Pasta, squash and feta salad with
olive dressing
Pear gingerbread
Pepper 'n' spice chicken
Refrigerator chocolate cake
Roquefort and walnut tart
Salsas
Souvlaki with cracked wheat salad
Stuffed picnic loaf
The perfect picnic text

Clare Ferguson
Fougasse
Hoummus
Tapenade
Taramasalata

Fran Warde
Chicken and tarragon pesto pasta
Chicken sticks with sweet chilli
Chickpea, tomato and pepper salad
Market picnic text
Nutty toffee apples and toffee cherries

Linda Collister
Fudge brownies
Toffee loaf cake

PHOTOGRAPHS
Key: r=right, l=left, c=centre

Ian Wallace endpapers; 3; 5; 11;
13–18; 21–22; 25; 29–30; 33; 36;
39; 43; 46–51; 55–58; 62–63
Debi Treloar 1–2; 4l, cr, r; 8–10;
28; 32; 38; 40; 42; 44–45; 60–61
Christopher Drake 4cl; 6; 19; 23
Martin Brigdale 26; 52
Peter Cassidy 34
Vanessa Davies 59